pig

CW00342119

For Euan and Winston

First published in 2005 by New Holland Publishers (NZ) Ltd
Auckland • Sydney • London • Cape Town

218 Lake Road, Northcote, Auckland, New Zealand
14 Aquatic Drive, Frenchs Forest, NSW 2086, Australia
86-88 Edgware Road, London, W2 2EA, United Kingdom
80 McKenzie Street, Cape Town 8001, South Africa

www.newhollandpublishers.co.nz

ISBN: 1 86966 095 1

Packaged for New Holland Publishers by
 Renaissance Publishing, Auckland
Design: Trevor Newman

A catalogue record for this book is available from the National
Library of New Zealand

10 9 8 7 6 5 4 3 2 1

Colour reproduction by SC (Sang Choy) International Pte Ltd,
 Singapore
Printed in China through Phoenix Offset, Hong Kong

pig tales

DON DONOVAN

NEW HOLLAND

In the beginning, the universe was created. This made a lot of people very angry, and has been widely regarded as a bad idea.

DOUGLAS ADAMS

Never tell your mum her diet's not working.

JOEL (14)

I learned long ago never to wrestle with a pig.

You get dirty, and besides, the pig likes it. CYRUS CHING

I think Bush is sitting on his brains.

NAOMI CUMMINGS

Any clod can have the facts; having opinions is an art.

CHARLES MCCABE

It has been my experience that folks who have no vices have very few virtues.

ABRAHAM LINCOLN

**Sex is hereditary.
If your parents never
had it, chances are
you won't either.**

JOSEPH FISCHER

We are all of us stars and we all deserve to twinkle.

MARILYN MONROE

Why is it when we talk to God we're praying – but when God talks to us, we're schizophrenic?

LILY TOMLIN

All of us are crazy in one way or another.

YIDDISH PROVERB

**Pigs is Pigs in China
And Pigs is Pigs in Cork
But Pigs Ain't Pigs in frying pans
Because there Pigs is Pork.**

ELLIS PARKER BUTLER

I like pigs. Dogs look up to us. Cats look down on us. Pigs treat us as equals.

WINSTON S. CHURCHILL

**Life is a tragedy when
seen in close-up, but a comedy
in long-shot.**

CHARLIE CHAPLIN

If you never change your mind, why have one?

EDWARD DE BONO

Life is too important to be taken seriously.

OSCAR WILDE

Strangers are just friends

waiting to happen. ANONYMOUS

If the Bible had said that Jonah swallowed the whale, I would believe it.

WILLIAM JENNINGS BRYAN

Imagination is the one weapon in the war against reality.

JULES DE GAULTIER

We'd have split up long ago but neither of us wanted custody of the child.

DEASIL WIDDERSHINS

You can say what you
like about long dresses,
but they cover a
multitude of shins.

MAE WEST

Bertie was a pig of action. 'Deeds, not grunts,' was his motto.

KENNETH GRAHAME

Paradise is exactly like where you are right now ... only much, much better.

LAURIE ANDERSON

Australia is an outdoor country. People only go indoors to use the toilet, and that's only a recent development.

BARRY HUMPHRIES

Adults are obsolete children.

DR SEUSS

**If we do not succeed,
then we run the risk of failure.**

DAN QUAYLE

Never invest in anything that eats or needs repairing.

BILLY ROSE

Don't let anybody tell you you are wasting your time when you're gazing into space ...

STEPHEN VIZINCZEY

I am free of all prejudices.
I hate everyone equally.

W.C. FIELDS

Only vegetables are happy.

WILLIAM FAULKNER

The cure for boredom is curiosity.

There is no cure for curiosity. ELLEN PARR

There are things that are so serious that you can only joke about them.

HEISENBERG

There is no gravity.
The earth sucks.

GRAFFITO

Life is like a dogsled team. If you ain't

the lead dog, the scenery never changes.

LEWIS GRIZZARD

Don't accept your dog's admiration as conclusive evidence that you are wonderful.

ANN LANDERS

Accidents will happen in the best regulated families.

PROVERB

**True happiness arises,
in the first place,
from the enjoyment of one's self,
and in the next,
from the friendship and
conversation of a few select
companions.**

JOSEPH ADDISON

I don't say we all ought to misbehave, but we ought to look as if we could.

ORSON WELLES

'Are we going to be friends forever?' asked Piglet.
'Even longer,' Pooh answered.

A.A. MILNE

If this raised a laugh, then try these
other titles by Don Donovan

Chewing the Cud   1 86966 068 4
Fowl Play   1 86966 094 3
Woolly Wisdom   1 86966 063 3